Pasta Party

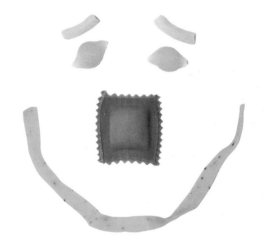

Written by Jack Hastings
Photography by Michael Curtain

sundance Newbridge

I like pasta.
Everyone in my family likes pasta.
We eat pasta all the time.

My dad likes square pasta.

We eat square pasta
on Monday night.

My mom likes tube pasta.

We eat tube pasta
on Tuesday night.

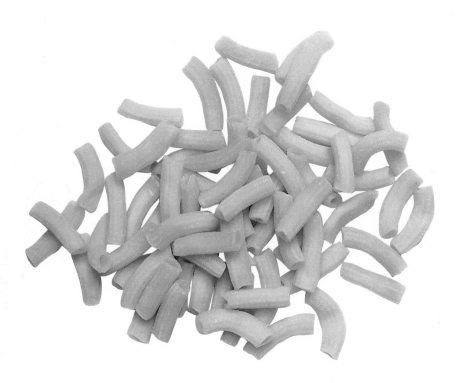

My baby brother
likes long pasta.

We eat long pasta
on Wednesday night.

My sister likes round pasta.

We eat round pasta
on Thursday night.

My grandpa likes flat pasta.

We eat flat pasta
on Friday night.

13

I like shell pasta.

We eat shell pasta
on Saturday night.

15

We have a pasta party
on Sunday night.